A TRUE BOOK™

T0011442

GREEN HOMES

Felicia Brower

Children's Press®
An imprint of Scholastic Inc.

Content Consultant
Jeslin Varghese, LEED AP, WELL AP
President & Director of Sustainability
GBRI

Library of Congress Cataloging-in-Publication Data
Names: Brower, Felicia, author.
Title: Green homes / Felicia Brower.
Description: First edition. | New York : Children's Press, an imprint of Scholastic Inc., 2024. | Series: A true book: a green future | Includes bibliographical references and index. | Audience: Ages 8–10. | Audience: Grades 4–6. | Summary: "This STEM-based set of True Books introduces students to the engineering innovations that can help us reach more environmentally friendly goals"— Provided by publisher.
Identifiers: LCCN 2023018940 (print) | LCCN 2023018941 (ebook) | ISBN 9781339020846 (library binding) | ISBN 9781339020853 (paperback) | ISBN 9781339020860 (ebk)
Subjects: LCSH: Ecological houses—Juvenile literature. | Architecture, Domestic—Environmental aspects—Juvenile literature. | Sustainable architecture—Juvenile literature. | BISAC: JUVENILE NONFICTION / Science & Nature / Environmental Conservation & Protection | JUVENILE NONFICTION / Science & Nature / Earth Sciences / General
Classification: LCC TH4860 .B76 2024 (print) | LCC TH4860 (ebook) | DDC 728/.047—dc23/eng/20230426
LC record available at https://lccn.loc.gov/2023018940
LC ebook record available at https://lccn.loc.gov/2023018941

10 9 8 7 6 5 4 3 2 1   24 25 26 27 28
Printed in China 62
First edition, 2024

Design by Kathleen Petelinsek
Series produced by Spooky Cheetah Press

Front cover: The concept design for "aquascrapers" of the future. Turn to page 32 to learn more.

Find the Truth!

Everything you are about to read is true *except* for one of the sentences on this page.

Which one is **TRUE**?

T or F   Some green homes are smaller than a parking spot.

T or F   Green homes cannot be built from natural resources like wood.

Find the answers in this book.

What's in This Book?

The **BIG** Truth

Wind power is a clean energy source.

Small changes can make your home greener.

2 Types of Green Homes

3 Green Homes of the Future

Plants can help skyscrapers save energy.

INTRODUCTION

It takes a lot of resources to build a home. **Wood**, **concrete**, and **metal** are common construction materials. **Paint**, **flooring**, **appliances**, and **furniture** are used inside the home, and **landscaping** is often added outside.

Burning **fossil fuels** releases **greenhouse gases** like carbon dioxide into the atmosphere.

An increase in greenhouse gases is linked to **climate change.**

It takes a lot of resources to run our homes as well. Heating and air-conditioning consume a lot of energy. So do lights and appliances. Most of that energy is generated by burning fossil fuels. **Water** is another important resource that plays a big role in our everyday lives. We use it to shower, do laundry, water our lawns, and more. All the **resources** we consume—**and waste**— have a big impact on our environment.

The **good news** is that people have become invested in making their homes more **sustainable**. That is where **green homes** come in! A green home is a house that is built or remodeled to **minimize its impact** on the environment. From design to construction to everyday life, green homes use as many **sustainable resources** as possible.

A person's carbon footprint is the amount of carbon dioxide that is generated from their actions.

These houses in Austin, Texas, have solar panels installed on their roofs. Solar panels create clean electricity.

Green homes are also designed to conserve resources like energy and water. By avoiding the use of toxic chemicals, green homes offer **healthier living environments**. Materials used in green homes are often recycled or **upcycled**, which reduces or avoids waste. There are many ways to make a house green. Read on to find out how!

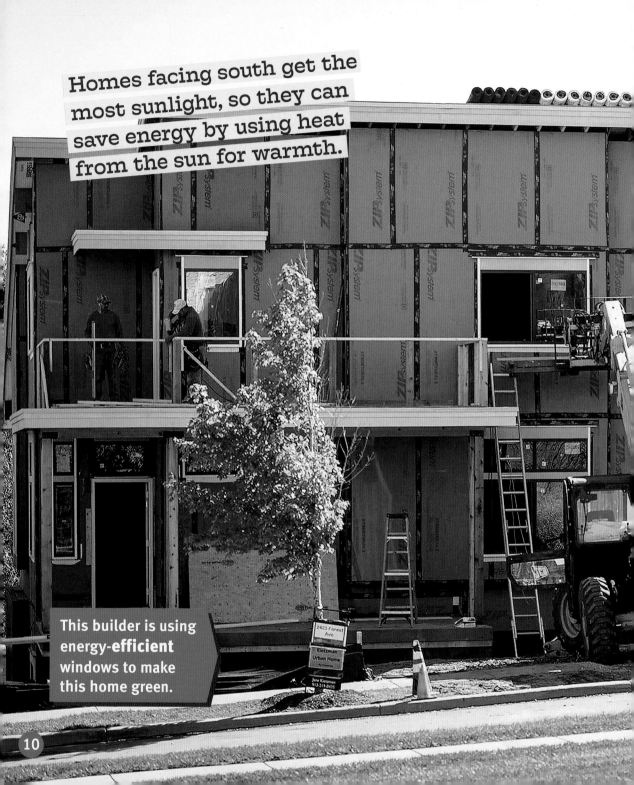

Homes facing south get the most sunlight, so they can save energy by using heat from the sun for warmth.

This builder is using energy-**efficient** windows to make this home green.

CHAPTER 1

Getting to Green

No matter what type of dwelling you live in, conserving resources can make your home greener. When constructing a green home, builders try to make sure every step of the process is sustainable. For example, they may build the home close to stores and businesses. Then the homeowners will not have to drive far to shop or go to work. They might even be able to walk. That means less fossil fuel is used by cars—and that is good for the environment!

Smart Construction Choices

Using materials from local sources means less fuel is needed to transport them to the construction site. Then fewer greenhouse gases are released into the air. Choosing wood—like bamboo—from sustainably harvested forests is one good choice for a green building material. Stone is another. It lasts a long time and is good at holding in heat.

Heat and cold air inside the home can escape

through walls, the roof, and even gaps around windows and doors. This energy loss can be lessened by sealing the gaps around windows and doors, and by using insulation.

On average, we lose one-third of our homes' heat through windows and doors.

Lessons from the Past

Hundreds of years ago, people started using walls made of rammed earth or straw bales to insulate their homes. Both methods are great at providing insulation, they don't create greenhouse gases, and they are renewable.

Rammed earth structures are created by ramming a mix of gravel, sand, clay, and similar materials between panels to form walls. The thick rammed earth walls absorb and release heat to keep the indoor temperature steady.

Straw walls are made by stacking up bales of straw and then covering them with plaster. Straw can also be made into insulation panels that are placed inside walls.

This photo shows what straw walls look like before they are covered.

The multistory homes in Sanaa, Yemen, are made from rammed earth.

Healthier Options

Some materials and products in our homes are made with volatile organic compounds (VOCs). Those are toxic chemicals found in things like paint, carpets, furniture, and cleaners. Over time, these chemicals can evaporate into the air, which is known as "off-gassing." To make our homes greener, we can choose products that are made with low or no VOCs. Or we can choose natural alternatives instead. These products and materials have fewer chemicals, making homes healthier to live in.

Some companies make natural paints that don't contain any VOCs.

Apps can help us control energy use in our homes—even when we're not there.

Save Your Energy

Energy-efficient features can make your home greener by reducing the amount of energy needed for everyday life. Things like LED light bulbs, Energy Star–certified appliances, and efficient heating, ventilation, and air-conditioning (HVAC) systems help keep electricity usage low. The more energy-efficient features a home has, the greener it is.

Native plants have adjusted to the environment. They don't need extra water to stay alive.

Conserving Water

Conserving water is important, especially now that climate change has made **droughts** more frequent. We can prevent water waste by installing special showerheads, toilets, faucets, and other plumbing fixtures designed to minimize water use. To conserve water outside the house, we can plant native plants instead of grass. Native plants are those that grow naturally in an area. They do not need to be watered as frequently as lawns do.

Reusing Water

Rainwater can be captured in rain barrels so it can be used around the house. Captured rainwater is often used for watering lawns and gardens and washing cars. Downspouts are pipes that drain rainwater from a roof. They can funnel rainwater runoff into containers or swales, which are low or sunken ditch-like areas. Swales slow the flow of water, making it easier for plants to absorb it, together with its minerals and nutrients.

Captured water is not for drinking.

Swale

Downspout

Rain barrel

Second Chances

Upcycling is when we take a product we would usually throw away and use it to create something useful. For example, a used milk carton can be turned into a bird feeder. Recycling is when waste is sent to a special facility to be converted into a new material. Carpets can be made from recycled plastic, and countertops from recycled glass. Almost everything we need in a house can be made from recycled materials! Both upcycling and recycling keep waste out of landfills. Green homes try to maximize their use.

Reducing Waste

Cutting back on the amount of waste we generate is just as important as recycling or upcycling. And it is an important part of living in a green home. We can use reusable grocery bags, avoid single-use food and drink containers, and donate things we no longer need instead of throwing them away. We can also compost food scraps, grass clippings, and dried leaves. Nutrient-rich compost makes a great addition to the soil in your indoor flowerpots or your garden.

Composting is a great way to reduce food waste.

Power Up!

Most electricity for homes is supplied by power plants that run on coal or natural gas. But some homes use energy from renewable sources to create all or part of their own electricity and heating and cooling. These alternative energies reduce the impact of the house on the environment. Here are three popular options:

SOLAR POWER: Solar panels are placed on the roof of a home. They are formed by several photovoltaic (PV) cells arranged together. The PV cells absorb sunlight and turn it into electricity. Then a device called an inverter transforms it into electricity that can be used in the home.

WIND POWER:

A residential wind turbine has blades that spin when the wind blows. That powers a rotor, which spins a small **generator** to create electricity. The electricity passes through an inverter so it can be used in the home.

Homes that are not connected to power plants at all are known as "off grid."

GEOTHERMAL POWER:

A geothermal pump can be used to heat and cool a home. It pumps water, or a liquid called a refrigerant, through a loop of underground pipes. Magma under Earth's crust heats the liquid, which is then pumped up through the house to heat the air inside. The system works the opposite way for cooling. The liquid absorbs the heat from the air inside the home and carries it underground.

A green home is healthier for the environment and for the people who live in it.

Plants grown on balconies can make skyscrapers greener.

2

Types of Green Homes

As you have read, there are lots of ways to make a home greener. There are also specific types of homes that are considered green. These homes come in a wide variety of sizes and shapes and they may be built with different materials. But they are all built with the goal of reducing their impact on the environment and creating a healthier living experience.

There are even kit homes that homeowners can put together themselves.

Prefabs are like a 3D puzzle you can live in!

Made to Order

Prefabricated homes, or "prefabs," are made in a factory. Then they are taken to the construction site to be put together. Prefab factories use computerized machines to cut all the materials so there is hardly any waste. There are two important things to consider, though. How eco-friendly a prefab is depends on the building company. And because the parts of these homes are built in advance, it can be hard to make changes after construction begins.

Saving Steel

Shipping containers are big steel boxes used to transport cargo on trains, trucks, and boats. Shipping containers that can no longer be used for transport can be upcycled into a container home. That is good for the environment because it reduces the need for new materials, like lumber or steel. And it keeps the old containers out of landfills.

This home in Malaysia is made of several recycled shipping containers that have been crafted together.

Think Small

A house made from only one shipping container is an example of a tiny or microhome. Tiny homes and microhomes are typically 100 to 600 square feet (9 to 56 square meters). The average is about 225 square feet (21 square meters). That's smaller than some parking spots! The smaller a home is, the less energy it needs to use for heating, cooling, and lighting. That's why people who are looking for a green home often think small.

This tiny house has lots of windows that let in sunlight and heat.

Space has to be used efficiently in a tiny home.

Live Differently

Living in a very small space often causes people to reduce their carbon footprint even further. There is no extra space in a tiny home, so people living there can't have a lot of belongings. They also have to think about how much waste they create every day or they'll simply run out of space. This type of lifestyle can take some getting used to, but it is a very environmentally friendly way to live.

This passive house is in Stamford, Connecticut.

Perfectly Passive

A passive house is one that stays warm in winter and cool in summer without using energy-consuming heating or cooling systems. It uses some techniques you have already read about. These homes are usually compact, and they have good insulation. They may be positioned so that in winter, maximum sunlight streams in through the windows to help warm the house. They may be built with shading devices—like overhangs—that keep the sun out in summer.

Going All Natural

Earthships are another type of green home. They are built using only natural and repurposed materials like reclaimed wood, adobe, recycled bottles, and tires. Earthships are designed with passive heating and cooling methods and don't use electric heat, fossil fuels, or wood. Earthships are part of a sustainable living environment, so water is collected for reuse and food is grown at home.

Large, south-facing windows are part of this earthship's design.

Finding a Balance

The most sustainable green homes are considered net zero or zero carbon. In a net-zero home, the amount of greenhouse gases produced is the same as the amount reduced through energy conservation. They cancel each other out. So the net sum of greenhouse gases is zero.

Timeline: Eco Milestones in the United States

1884
The first solar panels are installed on a New York City rooftop.

APRIL 22, 1970
The first Earth Day is celebrated in the United States.

1970s
The "Reduce, Reuse, Recycle" slogan is popularized to encourage eco-friendly habits.

JUNE 20, 1979
President Jimmy Carter has 32 solar panels installed on the White House roof.

A Zero Everyone Will Love

A zero-carbon home goes one step further. It is so energy efficient that it doesn't produce any greenhouse gases at all. Both net-zero and zero-carbon homes may also remove more **emissions** from the atmosphere than they **emit**. In that case, they are "net positive."

Carbon dioxide accounts for about 76 percent of all greenhouse gas emissions.

1992
The Environmental Protection Agency launches the Energy Star program to identify and promote energy-efficient products.

APRIL 22, 1993
President Bill Clinton announces the "Greening of the White House" initiative. Changes lead to 845 metric tons of carbon emissions being eliminated each year during his presidency.

1994
LEED (Leadership in Energy and Environmental Design) standards are introduced. LEED is the most widely used green building rating system in the world.

There are already more than 1.6 million certified green homes around the world.

This is a concept design for "aquascrapers." These buildings would be 100 percent sustainable—and mostly underwater!

Green Homes of the Future

In the future, we will see more and more homes built to be green, or remodeled to be greener! There are certifications offered by government agencies and private organizations that indicate how green a home is, and more homes will have them in the future. Let's take a look at one of these certifications, as well as what sustainable housing of the future will be.

Green Certified

LEED (Leadership in Energy and Environmental Design) is the most widely used certification system in the world. To become certified, a building is rated on the materials used in construction, water efficiency, energy efficiency, waste reduction, improved indoor air quality, and more. The more efficient a building is, the higher its rating. Those ratings are tied to different levels of certification: Certified, Silver, Gold, and Platinum. Platinum is the highest.

This home is LEED Platinum—certified.

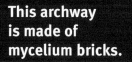

This archway is made of mycelium bricks.

Mycelium bricks can be grown in as little as five days.

The Future Is in Fungi

Scientists are experimenting with building materials made of fungi. When a mushroom grows in the woods, we see just the top part. Underneath is a huge collection of roots, known as mycelium. Certain types of mycelium can be used to make building materials that are water-, mold-, and fire-resistant.

When mycelium is grown in or around certain materials and is then heated and dried, it can be turned into insulation panels or bricks in a variety of shapes and sizes. Mycelium grows very quickly and is 100 percent natural and renewable. It's also **biodegradable**, making it a zero-waste product.

Roofs that are covered in plants are known as living green roofs.

Plant Life

Concrete and asphalt absorb and emit more heat from the sun than trees and grass do. That is why city centers are often called heat islands. Usually people combat the heat by using air conditioners. But now there's a better way. Some city buildings cover their roofs in plants—and more will do so in the future. The plants absorb the sun's energy and become natural insulators for buildings as they grow. The leaves provide shade, which also helps beat the heat.

Reaching Higher

Many cities might not have a lot of green space. But they do have skyscrapers—which can be very green indeed. Tall buildings have access to more sunlight, which makes solar power a great option. And the higher up you go, the more constant the wind is, so wind power is a great option as well. In the future, more buildings will be built with solar panels and wind turbines.

These twin towers in Bahrain are connected by three wind turbines, which provide up to 15 percent of the building's power.

Super Skyscrapers

The Bank of America Tower in New York City was the first new commercial skyscraper in the United States to get a LEED Platinum certification. It uses wind turbines, solar panels, and **biofuel** to create enough energy to meet 70 percent of its annual electric needs. Shanghai Tower in China is also LEED Platinum–certified. It has rainwater collection systems, sky gardens, more than 200 wind turbines, plus additional energy-saving measures to reduce fossil fuels usage and waste.

The Bank of America Tower also collects and reuses its water—which saves about 100 million gallons per year!

Bank of America Tower, New York

Shanghai Tower, China

Going for Green

In the future, our homes will be smaller, more energy efficient, and healthier—and our carbon footprints will get smaller. This will help slow climate change. That's great news for the planet and everyone living on it. And now that you know more about sustainable practices, you can make your home as green as possible too! Sustainable homes are changing the world for the better, and it is in your hands to contribute to this change!

The Ecocapsule

The Ecocapsule is a microhome designed by a company in Slovakia, Europe, called Nice Architects. It is completely self-sufficient, fairly easy to transport, and can be placed anywhere in the world! Take a look at its features:

Its small size, measuring a little over 15 feet (4.6 meters) long and 7 feet (2.1 meters) wide, reduces energy use.

Solar cells on the roof produce electricity during the day.

The oval shape minimizes heat loss and makes water easily flow off its roof.

A rainwater collection system accumulates rainwater in a tank, where it will be filtered for personal use.

A low-noise wind turbine can produce electricity 24 hours a day. Its pole can be folded for easy transport.

Interior space-saving features include a tiny kitchenette and a foldaway bed.

The bathroom features a water-saving faucet and showerhead. The toilet doesn't use any water.

Take Action

A Greener Home

There are lots of easy ways you can start making your home greener. Here are a few ideas.

TO SAVE WATER:

✔ Turn off the water while you brush your teeth.

✔ Wet your hands and then turn off the faucet to wash them. Turn the water back on to rinse.

✔ Take quick showers instead of baths.

Ask an adult to help:

✔ Look for leaky faucets and fix them.

✔ If your plumbing fixtures need an update, install products designed to minimize water use.

TO SAVE ELECTRICITY AND HEAT:

- ✔ Turn off the lights when you leave a room.
- ✔ Turn off the TV when you're finished watching.
- ✔ Unplug chargers when they're not in use.
- ✔ Put on a sweater instead of turning up the heat in winter, and wear shorts instead of turning on the AC in summer.

Ask an adult to help:

- ✔ Feel around the windows for gaps or blowing air where heat might be escaping. Seal the gaps.
- ✔ Swap out traditional light bulbs with LEDs to boost your energy efficiency.
- ✔ Keep the house at a steady temperature to use less energy for heating and cooling.

True Statistics

Estimated percentage of greenhouse gas emissions that come from buildings in the United States: **almost 40**

U.S. homes with easy-to-fix leaks: 5 to 10 percent

Amount of water wasted in one year from a leaky faucet that drips at the rate of one drop per second: 3,000 gallons

Average amount of energy LEED projects save compared to non-green homes: 20 to 30 percent

Energy saved using energy-efficient light bulbs compared to regular bulbs: 75 percent

Number of continents with LEED-certified homes: 6 (none in Antarctica . . . yet!)

Did you find the truth?

T Some green homes are smaller than a parking spot.

F Green homes cannot be built from natural resources like wood.

Resources

Other books in this series:

You can also look at:

Aloian, Molly. *Living Green at Home*. New York: Crabtree Publishing, 2013.

Grunbaum, Mara. *Understanding Climate Change: The Greenhouse Effect*. New York: Children's Press, 2020.

Leedy, Loreen. *The Shocking Truth about Energy*. New York: Holiday House, 2011.

Taylor, Saranne. *Green Homes*. New York: Crabtree Publishing, 2014.

Glossary

biodegradable (bye-oh-di-GRAY-duh-buhl) able to be broken down by natural processes

biofuel (BYE-oh-fyoo-uhl) fuel that is made from renewable materials such as plants or animal waste

climate change (KLYE-mit CHAYNJ) global warming and other changes in the weather and weather patterns that are happening because of human activity

droughts (DROUTS) long periods without rain

efficient (i-FISH-uhnt) working or operating well and without waste

emissions (i-MISH-uhnz) substances released into the atmosphere

emit (i-MIT) to produce or send out something such as heat, light, signals, or sound

fossil fuels (FAH-suhl FYOO-uhlz) coal, oil, or natural gas formed from the remains of prehistoric plants and animals

generator (JEN-uh-ray-tur) a machine that produces electricity by turning a magnet inside a coil of wire

greenhouse gases (GREEN-hous GAS-ez) gases such as carbon dioxide and methane that contribute to the greenhouse effect

sustainable (suh-STAY-nuh-buhl) done in a way that can be continued and that doesn't use up natural resources

upcycled (UHP-sye-kuhld) turned into something more valuable

Index

Page numbers in **bold** indicate illustrations.

About the Author

Felicia Brower is a writer living in Denver, Colorado, who is passionate about sustainability and green living. She studied environmental policy and planning at Virginia Tech and loves learning about and sharing ways to protect the environment.